My Hygiene

By

Kirsty Holmes

CRABTREE PUBLISHING COMPANY
WWW.CRABTREEBOOKS.COM

Published in Canada
Crabtree Publishing
616 Welland Avenue
St. Catharines, ON
L2M 5V6

Published in the United States
Crabtree Publishing
PMB 59051
350 Fifth Ave, 59th Floor
New York, NY 10118

Published by Crabtree Publishing Company in 2019

All rights reserved. No part of this publication may be reproduced, stored in a retrieval system or be transmitted in any form or by any means, electronic, mechanical, photocopying, recording, or otherwise, without the prior written permission of the copyright owner.

©2018 BookLife Publishing

Author: Kirsty Holmes

Editors: Holly Duhig, Janine Deschenes

Design: Jasmine Pointer

Proofreader: Melissa Boyce

Production coordinator and prepress technician (interior): Margaret Amy Salter

Prepress technician (covers): Ken Wright

Print coordinator: Katherine Berti

Photographs
All images from Shutterstock

Printed in the U.S.A./122018/CG20181005

Library and Archives Canada Cataloguing in Publication

Holmes, Kirsty, author
    My hygiene / Kirsty Holmes.

(Our values)
Includes index.
Issued in print and electronic formats.
ISBN 978-0-7787-5422-0 (hardcover).--
ISBN 978-0-7787-5445-9 (softcover).--
ISBN 978-1-4271-2217-9 (HTML)

    1. Hygiene--Juvenile literature. I. Title.

RA780.H65 2018   j613   C2018-905475-1
                                      C2018-905476-X

Library of Congress Cataloging-in-Publication Data

Names: Holmes, Kirsty, author.
Title: My hygiene / Kirsty Holmes Crabtree.
Description: New York, New York : Crabtree Publishing Company, 2019. |
Series: Our values | Includes index.
Identifiers: LCCN 2018043783 (print) | LCCN 2018043947 (ebook) |
  ISBN 9781427122179 (Electronic) |
  ISBN 9780778754220 (hardcover) |
  ISBN 9780778754459 (paperback)
Subjects: LCSH: Hygiene--Juvenile literature.
Classification: LCC RA780 (ebook) | LCC RA780 .H66 2019 (print) |
  DDC 613--dc23
LC record available at https://lccn.loc.gov/2018043783

Contents

Page 4   What Is Hygiene?
Page 6   We Need Clean Skin
Page 8   Dirt and Germs
Page 10 Wash Your Hands
Page 12 Baths and Showers
Page 14 Clean All Over
Page 16 Brush Your Teeth
Page 18 Cleaning Up
Page 20 Stop the Spread!
Page 24 Glossary and Index

Words that look like **this** can be found in the glossary on page 24.

What Is Hygiene?

Hygiene means keeping ourselves and our **surroundings** clean. Having good hygiene is very important.

When we have good hygiene, our bodies are clean. This helps us stay healthy. It can also help us feel happy.

We Need Clean Skin

Our skin helps our bodies stay healthy.

Our skin has a job to do. It protects our bodies from things that could make us sick. It helps keep them from getting inside our bodies.

When our skin is not clean, it cannot do its job well.

Use soap and water to clean your skin.

Dirt and Germs

Messy play can be fun. But it is important to clean our skin afterward.

Dirt can make our skin unclean. It includes things such as mud and dust.

Germs are tiny living things that can make you sick. They live in things like dirt or old food. Our skin helps keep germs out of our bodies. Having good hygiene means that we help keep germs out.

Wash Your Hands

Washing your hands is very important. It is one way you can wash away germs from your skin.

Baths and Showers

Don't forget to clean your toes!

We can clean the rest of our bodies by bathing, or taking baths and showers. These help to get rid of germs—and bad smells!

Playing sports can make you sweaty. To stay clean, bathe afterward!

Children should bathe at least once or twice a week, or whenever they are dirty, **sweaty**, or have been swimming. Don't forget to wash your hair, too!

Clean All Over

To have good hygiene, we need to keep all of our body parts clean. Germs can get inside parts like our ears and mouths. It is important to clean them **regularly**.

Your hands touch a lot of different things every day! Don't forget to clean your fingers and under your fingernails. Ask an adult to trim your fingernails and toenails when they are long.

Brush Your Teeth

Food can get stuck in our teeth when we eat.

It is important to keep our mouths and teeth clean. Dirt and germs are bad for our teeth and can make our breath smell bad.

We need to floss our teeth, too! Flossing gets rid of anything stuck in our teeth.

Brush your teeth for two minutes twice a day. Use a toothbrush and toothpaste. Make sure you brush the front and back of every tooth!

Cleaning Up

Having good hygiene means we keep the places around us, such as our homes, clean. Germs can live on dirty plates, cups, and **cutlery**. They need to be washed after they are used.

Clothes should be washed when they are dirty.

Our clothing can get dirty and sweaty. We should change our clothing every day. Wearing clean clothing helps us stay healthy, and smell pleasant to others.

Stop the Spread!

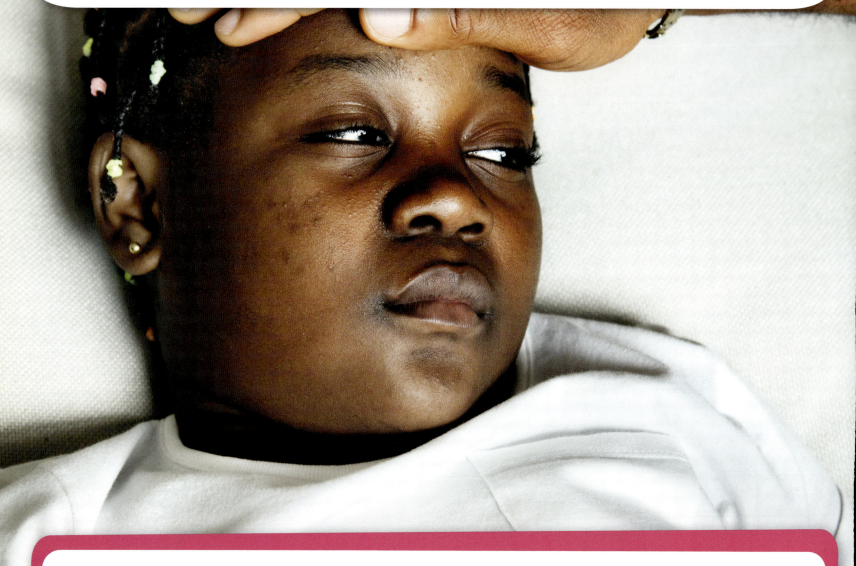

Part of having good hygiene is making sure you do not spread germs when you are ill.

If you cough or sneeze, you can spread your germs to other people and make them ill too.

Try to "catch" coughs and sneezes in your sleeve or in a tissue.

Used tissues are full of germs! Make sure you throw them in the garbage.

Hand sanitizer gel can also kill germs.

Wash your hands after you cough or sneeze.

Glossary

cutlery — Knives, forks, and spoons
hand sanitizer gel — Gel that kills germs
regularly — To do something often, usually at the same time or on the same day
surroundings — The area around you, such as your room
sweaty — When a person's body releases sweat, which is moisture that cools us down

Index

clothes 19
dirt, dirty 8–9, 13, 16, 18–19
food 9, 16
germs 8–10, 12, 14, 16, 18, 20–23
illness 20–23
skin 6–10
soap and water 7, 11
washing 10–11, 13, 18–19, 23